GENTLE GIANT

At Sea with the Humpback Whale

TSUNEO NAKAMURA

CHRONICLE BOOKS

SAN FRANCISCO

First published in the United States 1988 by
Chronicle Books

Printed in Hong Kong.

First published in Japan by Heibonsha, Limited, Publishers, Tokyo.

Library of Congress Cataloging-in-Publication Data

Nakamura, Tsuneo, 1949–
    Gentle giant.

    Translation of: Kujira
    1. Humpback whale.   2. Humpback whale—Pictorial
works.   3. Mammals—Pictorial works.   I. Title.
QL737.C424N3513   1988   599.51   87-35310
ISBN 0-87701-506-6 (pbk.)

Edited by Heidi Fritschel
Cover design by Julie Noyes

Distributed in Canada by
Raincoast Books
8680 Cambie Street
Vancouver, British Columbia V6P 6M9
10   9   8   7   6   5

Chronicle Books
275 Fifth Street
San Francisco, California
94103

FOREWORD

In the winter season, when breeding and calving take place, the humpbacks assemble in the warm, clear, tropical waters of the world's oceans. In Hawaii, the assembly grounds lie near or between the major islands, and the whales may easily be seen from shore or boat. The near presence of one of these whales, fifteen meters or more in length, and perhaps thirty tons in weight, is awesome; their magnificent leaps from the water and the thunder of their tails slapping the surface emphasize our own fragility. But when we enter the water and swim with them, it is their grace, serenity, and curiosity that impress us. There is a special feeling in being studied by the eye of a whale as the animal glides by, gently raising its long, white-bottomed flipper above your head, aware of you, and accepting. At times, when underwater with the whales, the song reverberates with such force that one's body begins to resonate with each deep tone. A calf rolls at the surface, seeming to dance to the song, its mother nearby, watchful. The singer rises to the surface, all male, and joins with the mother in a long courtship episode that may last for hours. Other males intrude to claim their rights and the peace is disturbed by the contest, prolonged and fierce. Then all is calm again and perhaps another precious calf begins in mother's womb. These experiences and impressions that I have had when with the whales can now be shared through the photographs of Tsuneo Nakamura, who has worked closely with us to observe these animals. And, as we study the humpback whale, and continue to learn more of its life and its intricate society, our appreciation of these powerful and graceful animals is enriched, and our concern for their welfare heightened.

Louis M. Herman

Kewalo Basin Marine Mammal Laboratory
University of Hawaii

PREFACE

In 1977 in Alaska's Glacier Bay, I saw the breaching of a humpback whale for the first time. I was so taken by surprise that quite unintentionally I cried out. Since that time, I have become very interested in whales, and whenever I hear that I can view them by going to the Bering Sea or the Arctic or Antarctic oceans or any ocean or sea around the world, I grab my camera and go. And no sooner had I begun to think that I wanted to meet whales in their underwater world than I became acquainted with Professor Louis Herman, and he let me join his whale project team at the University of Hawaii. Day after day, riding in a tiny rubber raft, we chased whales in the open seas around Hawaii from sunrise to sunset. In that way, I gathered my pictures of the humpback whales.

Gentleness Concealed in a Giant Body

February 6

The Aloha Airlines Boeing 737, only just lifted off from Honolulu Airport, readied for landing at Kahului Airport situated on the plain between Maui's Haleakala and Puukukui mountains. The seat belt light came on, and I figured that the plane was about to go in for a landing, when the pilot announced, "Whales on the right." The plane went into a sharp turn.

During the commotion among my fellow passengers, I rushed to the window to look down. I saw three whales swimming along beneath the surface, like three great shadows in the sea. While we all looked at the whales, the plane continued to circle around. As soon as the whales disappeared, the plane changed its position and landed at Kahului.

It was a good start for me, for I had just arrived in Hawaii to investigate humpback whales by joining the Marine Mammals Study Team of the University of Hawaii.

February 8

At 8:30 in the morning we arrived at Lahaina, formerly a whaling port. All the trawlers and whalers had left, and only a 3½-meter-long rubber raft, sitting off to the side, occupied the quiet port.

Near the raft was parked a station wagon several times bigger than the boat. The vehicle bore on its side the message: OFFICIAL USE ONLY, UNIVERSITY OF HAWAII. A pile of goods had been removed from the wagon: gasoline tanks, life preservers, a wireless radio, batteries, an underwater recorder, an antenna, a permit flag, camera bags, food, recording paper, oars, polytanks, diving instruments, and so on.

The marine survey team's membership for the day consisted of Tom, a lecturer at the university; a volunteer named Budgie; Jim from Earthwatch; and me. After a brief exchange of morning pleasantries, we began to load the equipment into the raft. I wondered if this tiny craft had sufficient capacity to hold the four of us plus the large load; for on top of all that gear, each of us had a sack containing a change of clothes, and I also had three underwater cameras, two regular cameras, a number of interchangeable lenses, and my diving equipment.

The load was somehow fit onto the floor of the boat, and we were all forced to make a seat for ourselves on the inflated pontoons that formed the sides of the craft, with our legs resting on the load.

Just on time at 9:00. With the raft full of people and equipment, we set out for the open sea. The sound of the raft's twenty-five-horsepower outboard motor echoed all around the port. Before us in the channel was Lanai Island, toward which we were slowly heading. To the right was Molokai, and to the left was Kahoolawe.

Under Tom's leadership, everyone was assigned an area of the ocean's surface to keep watch over. After all, no one could be sure just when and where a whale would spout or put in an appearance.

Here and there were floating other whale-watching boats filled with curious spectators. Although there were no doubt whales near those boats, we decided to look for our whales elsewhere.

We were only ten minutes into our run when Budgie cried out, "Two o'clock spray!" Everyone looked in the direction she was pointing, and there they were: two whales beginning their dives, their flukes (the lobes of their tails) raised high into the air. We immediately opened throttle and headed for the spot where the animals had dived. Our raft bucked over the churning surface while we all clung to the lanyards strung along the side of the small boat to keep from being dumped overboard.

Five minutes later, we arrived at the place where we estimated the whales had begun their dives, but of course there were no whales, nor even their shadows, to be found. So we cut the engine and waited for the whales to resurface.

Just twelve minutes after the first sighting, two whales spouted

500 meters ahead of us. Then another two appeared. It was a pod, or group, of four whales headed straight for Molokai. We recorded the amount of time the pod spent underwater when it dove and the distance it traversed, as well as the course the pod was taking. After starting up the engine, we followed the course the whales were taking and adjusted our speed to match that of the pod.

Ten more minutes passed, and Budgie murmured, "Just another few minutes. It'll be soon now." The four of us on the raft concentrated on the surface of the ocean that surrounded us.

Exactly twelve minutes later, two whales surfaced just 100 meters away from us; ten seconds later, the other two came up. The whales spouted three times, as they had before, and then dove back into the water. Throughout this time, I was standing on the violently bucking raft, frantically focusing my camera lenses, and taking shots of the whales' flukes (straight-on shots that could be used in identifying the animals).

I wondered if the time had at last arrived. I glanced over at Tom, and he, looking in the direction of my diving gear, nodded at me, telling me it was a go. Hurriedly, I removed the long-sleeved jacket and long pants I wore to protect myself from sunburn, and donned my diving gear.

I was tense with the mixed feelings that had welled up in me. The excitement at the thought that after a year's hiatus I would encounter whales beneath the ocean's surface once again was mingled with the trepidation I felt in the face of the whales' awesomeness and power. I put on my face mask, grabbed my camera, and, straddling the side of the raft, assumed a standby position. The raft was moving in concert with the whales' direction and speed. I imagined the great animals gliding along right under my legs.

Ten minutes, eleven minutes . . . . I was growing more and more tense. Controlling my breathing, I kept a lookout all around the raft. It had been exactly twelve minutes. Then, only twenty meters behind our raft, two whales broke the surface with a resounding "bwoosh." As soon as I heard it, I dove into the sea, with the raft continuing on ahead. The water around me was white with the bubbles from my breathing apparatus and from the raft's propeller. I immediately dove deeper, and as soon as I exited the curtain of bubbles, two great shadows passed together below my legs. They looked like submarines. The whales slid through the sea by moving their flukes slowly up and down and extending their flippers.

They were massive. Even though I was using a wide-angle lens, one whale extended beyond the camera's frame. In about two seconds, the heads of the two whales passed out of my view, and their flukes disappeared soon after. Exhilarated, I returned to the surface. As I was gaining my breath, I again heard "bwoosh" sounding all over the ocean, and the heads of the two whales came into view. Hurriedly, I dove back down. The whales threw a quick glance my way, but quietly they passed me by and again disappeared.

February 15

Tom shouted, "Floating whale!" When I turned my binoculars to where he was pointing, I found a whale floating with just a bit of its dorsal fin showing, looking almost like a wave. We brought our raft up quietly to within 200 meters of the whale, which was stretched out near the surface, its great length visible from blowhole to dorsal fin. Keeping its position, the whale breathed in and out a few times, making a noise but not spraying.

"It's probably a singing whale," Tom said. He unpacked the hydrophone and put it into the water. Through the earphones, I heard a sound like a cross between a purring cat and an angry pig, repeating itself over and over.

Within a quarter of an hour, the sound from the hydrophone grew louder. No sooner had Tom shouted, "The whale's coming up!" than the great animal rose to the surface, breaking through the water some 200 meters ahead of us.

After it had stretched itself and settled its breathing down as before, it cried out and sank into the water. I kept still and tried to listen carefully. Ever so gently, the whale's cry came to me through the water. I placed the oar, which we had brought along in case of engine trouble, into the water, just as the Eskimos do to listen for the sounds of seals. I could hear the whale's cry much more clearly as it resonated through the oar's handle.

Who on earth could describe the ocean as "the silent world," we wondered as we listened to the whale's voice. Meanwhile, the whale surfaced again as before.

I finished recording the whale's voice, prepared myself and my equipment for underwater photography, and slid quietly into the water. Holding my head above the water and without splashing, I swam slowly toward where the whale had sunk below the surface. Drenched in the ocean's waters, I heard the whale's strange ambiguous cries echoing louder and louder. When I looked back to the raft to see if I had swum far enough, Tom waved at me to continue. So I swam on, not only hearing the whale's song but actually feeling it throughout my whole body.

When I figured I had come close to where the whale had gone down, I was suddenly shaken by that booming sound we had heard before, as the whale crashed through the surface of the sea. I altered my threatened position and looked toward where the sound originated. Only thirty meters ahead of me, the whale was floating, its side turned toward me. I was maneuvering myself around to face the whale when it again headed down into the depths, its flukes fluttering before my eyes. I immediately gave a big kick with my flippers and dove after the whale. With my snorkeling gear I descended more than ten meters, but quickly lost the huge beast in the murky sea.

I resurfaced and decided to wait for the whale to come back up, listening to its song as I waited. Ten minutes passed and I was expecting it to come up at any minute.

Suddenly, two large open-sea sharks over three meters in length silently appeared and began to circle beneath my legs. "Danger!" I thought. Without taking my eyes off the sharks, I raised my left hand above the water and made a fist, a signal to those aboard the raft to come and get me. Meanwhile, the sharks drew closer, ever shrinking the diameter of their circling. They seemed to be moving convulsively, a known sign that a shark is closing in on its prey. I listened carefully for the approach of the boat, but I heard no engine sounds at all. At some point unnoticed by me, the whale had ceased its cries.

Desperately hoping that the raft would arrive quickly, I raised and lowered my hands in the air over and over, making the signal for rescue. My camera, which I had lifted out of the water, had grown heavy.

Suddenly, one shark stopped circling, and, coiling its body like a snake, rushed at me. I decided to photograph this shark that was, I thought, about to devour me. I readied my camera and took the shot. The shark slowed down just a bit, probably bothered by the click of the shutter. But it continued to come at me.

The shark's snout was only fifty centimeters or so away from me. I shouted, "Damn you!" and shoved my camera out at the monster, striking it squarely on its nose. Even so, I thought the shark had gotten a piece of me. But at the sound of the dull thud, the shark broke off its attack, took a U turn away from me, and, with its companion, disappeared into the sea's dark depths.

The danger had passed. As I raised my head above the water and calmed my breathing down, I heard the raft's engine start up and saw the small craft move toward me. When I looked up, my crewmates, who knew nothing of what had transpired beneath the surface of the water, were eyeing me quizzically as if to say "What happened?" Perhaps they thought I had driven the singing whale away. I shouted at them, "Sharks! Sharks! I was attacked by sharks!" At that, they all raised a commotion, and in an instant, I was pulled up into the raft.

February 19

It was 3 P.M. I was thinking that the morning and early afternoon had not been very productive. After departing Lahaina at 8:15 in the morning, we had not come across any whale pods, and I had had no opportunity for any more "fluke" shots.

We were all gazing aimlessly out to sea, almost ready to give it up for the day, thinking "Today's not a good day. Let's hope for tomorrow." But we kept on going, and the wind came up, blowing straight through Maui's deep valley in the peculiar way it does, partially roughening up the surface of the water, but leaving a clearly distinct area of calm. We were headed for Lanai, traveling over calm waters about fifty meters away from the rough stuff.

"Spray!" Jim yelled out. The sighting was about a mile away. It took us five minutes to get to the area. We shut down the engine and waited on the next spouting. Fifteen minutes . . . twenty minutes . . . nothing yet. The roughened water was swinging toward us; the wind was changing its direction.

Pierre murmured, "We must have lost it." We began to stow away the equipment that had been scattered around the bottom of the raft—cameras, underwater speaker, and diving gear—and prepared to head back to port. At that moment, it happened. "Whoa!" I blurted out. A huge black shadow hove into view only two or three meters below the surface.

On our raft, pandemonium: "It's a whale!" "It's a whale-shark!" "It's a submarine!" A few seconds later, flukes appeared above the water. By then, I had already jumped into my gear, grabbed my camera, and was diving into the water. The enormous flukes were waving up and down, as if they meant to stroke my face, even as they receded away from me. I went down deeper, swimming under the boat, and chased after the great beast. The whale made a U-turn, sank a little lower, and again came toward the raft.

"Good," I thought, and took a deep breath, intending to dive down and meet the whale face to face. The whale continued to come slowly in my direction, about ten meters below the surface. I grew impatient and started to take some photographs. The whale sped up a bit and sank deeper again. I knew whales did not like the sound of the camera's shutter, but my impatience got the better of me, and I shot anyway. I regretted my slip-up immediately.

Pierre, the raft's pilot, donned his mask and fins and came to join me. While we were exchanging eye signals, the whale drew closer again, to within fifteen meters right under us. Immediately, Pierre dove toward the whale. In order to get a picture of Pierre with the whale, I followed behind him, keeping my camera ready.

The whale did not seem to mind us, but started to slowly sink deeper into the sea. Out of breath, the two of us returned to the surface. We removed our snorkels and began to talk excitedly about what had just happened.

But rough seas came on fast, and a strong wind blew up around us. In an instant, the highly buoyant rubber raft had been blown away from us. On the raft, Jim and Ronnie did not know how to restart the engine and just looked at us helplessly over the side of the retreating raft. Pierre, still in his snorkeling equipment, swam with great vigor, chasing after the boat, with me following after.

After ten or fifteen minutes of swimming, I put my face up and looked in the direction the wind was blowing. The distance between the raft and me was not lessening. I could not increase my speed because of the resistance caused by my underwater camera. I was growing impatient, as well as a bit worried about the possible arrival of a shark upon this scene.

Meanwhile, Pierre at last reached the raft. I saw him being pulled up into the boat by the two others. Greatly relieved, I stopped swimming and struggling against the muscle strain that was coming on in my legs. I floated there on the surface. In about five minutes, I heard the engine draw close. As I climbed aboard, Jim and Ronnie welcomed me with faces lit up in smiles.

February 22

Five in the morning. I was awakened by the morning call bell. It was still very dark outside. Rubbing the sleep out of my eyes, I hurriedly got myself going. Within forty minutes, the car arrived at Lahaina. Already the staff from the university was loading our equipment into the raft. The night had not yet given way to dawn; by the lights of the harbor, I also loaded my gear—cameras and diving equipment—aboard the raft. Leaving a trail on the quiet sea-face of the lonely harbor, our raft headed toward the open sea. The jet-black figure of Haleakala was silhouetted against the freshly brightening morning sky.

During the night whales are barely active, and the pace of their breathing slows down remarkably to one breath every fifteen or twenty minutes. So the great animals are not easily seen. "Come on, whales," I wished to myself, "show us where you are." The sky continued to grow brighter.

I was afraid we had woken up so early in vain. I very much wanted to get a picture of a spouting whale backed by a dawning sky. The day before we had left port at 6:40 A.M., but it was not until 7:50, when the sun had fully risen over the top of the mountain, that we found any whales. During the daytime they showed themselves so much, I thought, why were we so unlucky in the early morning. We departed Lahaina and headed for Molokini.

"Spray!" The first person to call out was the Earthwatcher, the wife of Jim the reporter. The whale spouted a few times while floating on the surface, then kicked his flukes up high and dove into the water. I heard that familiar "bwoosh" sound again and turned to see two more whales spouting just 100 meters away. I realized that today I would be able to take as many pictures as I wanted before the sun rose over the mountain's shadow.

We moved a bit toward the open sea, and I readied my camera for some pictures of spouting whales against the deep black mountain shadow and the dawn-reddened sky. The first pod sprayed a few times, and at the moment they kicked their flukes up, a whale from another pod sent a plume of spray high into the sky. The scene from my imagination spread out to fill the viewfinder of my camera. Whales floated on the water's surface, taking in relaxed and leisurely breaths, and then submerged. I grew tired watching the ocean's surface, and then I heard the sound of a whale spouting once again and saw it all in the distance. Photography itself is rather easy, so I grew anxious and irritated waiting for an opportunity to take some early morning shots.

When the whale came up for the third time, the sun was shining through the clouds that floated over the mountain peak. And so ended this particular session of early morning photography.

February 25

"Beluga, Beluga, this is Noire." A weak voice, nearly obliterated by the engine's noise, reached out to us from the waterproof container. Hurriedly, Tom cut the engine, grabbed the mike, and responded, "This is Beluga. Hi, Gordon." From the speaker, Gordon's discernibly excited voice could be heard: "Right now over here in front of Olawalu, we have a really active pod of whales that should be excellent for photography. Get over here fast. They've been doing stuff like head-rises, breaching, and fluke slapping for awhile now. We're too busy to take any notes."

"Thanks, Gordon." Right away, Tom restarted the engine and headed toward Olawalu Point near Garbage Hill, where a field station is located. When we arrived at a point about two miles from shore, we saw a whale doing some violent fluke swishing. The strand along Olawalu Park was crowded with cars parked for whale viewing.

Our raft approached the area rapidly. The whales' actions were violent, and they were moving fast. When one whale surfaced and spouted, I saw that his flukes were sitting over the water at a strange angle. Before I had time to wonder what had happened, I noticed that another whale had surfaced right under the first whale and was pushing at the first whale's flukes with its head. The first whale was thus forced to bend its body unnaturally, so it started to push the other whale back down with its flukes. The body of the second whale was pushed down while its head stayed up. In this odd position, it could not help spouting while still partially submerged, and the water all around was filled with bubbling white foam.

After a bit, this whale was able to force its way to the surface, and as soon as it did so, its head was violently rocked. For the other whale was getting its revenge by whacking the interloper on the head with its great flukes, which burst out of the water beneath the victim's reeling head.

It was a terrible tumult. The whales were all scratched by the barnacles attached to their bodies. Right next to these struggling behemoths, another pair was colliding against each other, and with mouths full of sea water, they were repeatedly head slapping and blowing while underwater. In this way, they were intimidating each other. What an awesome sight!

As the whales zigzagged through the water, the gallery of cars along the shore moved accordingly. Along with the noises made by the whales' spouting and fluke slapping, I could hear the screams and yells coming from the shore.

The scene developing before my eyes was nothing less than a dynamic collision between these huge creatures. Often when I had dived into the water from the raft, the great whales had changed their course and run from me. But those former gentle giants certainly seemed like fierce and violent beasts right now. Over and over as they raced through the water, they banged together and withdrew and sank below the surface and rose again.

A trawler with four or five lines set out for marlin cut its engine and sat there halted by the sudden approach of the whales. Hurriedly, the fishermen reeled in their lines, as the whales swam once around their craft and headed again toward the shore.

Suddenly one of the whales rose halfway out of the water and breached. Tom murmured, "It's going to do it again." So I kept a close watch on the ocean's surface and carefully positioned my finger right above the shutter release. I looked all around the raft and had no idea where in the wide sea the whale was going to breach. Time passed so slowly. As I was waiting, thinking, standing with a line from the side of the raft wound around my waist, my head was scanning over the surface of the sea like a lighthouse.

"Bwoosh!" The tension aboard the raft snapped as the whale leaped out, breaking the sea's surface in two. I turned my camera lens in the direction of the sound, while focusing and firing, focusing and firing. The whale's back was toward me, and nearly its entire body was up in the air. It was a magnificent breach. As the third frame of the motor-driven film was exposed, I saw only white, frothy waves in the viewfinder.

After the breaching ended, the whales resumed rolling over each other, slapping each other with their flukes, and coursing through the water, their furious fighting unabated. I could not take my eyes from the finder. As I wondered what was going on, the color of the water's surface began to whiten, and a whale rose straight up out of the water, spouting as it came. At the same time, right near us, another whale was poking through the surface, but this one was visible only from its midsection to its flukes. The first whale pushed itself further out of the water while it continued to spout horizontally over the surface. The upside-down whale, on the other hand, suddenly slammed its flukes down, striking the first whale in the head. In blank amazement, I continued to poke at the shutter release, while in the finder, unbelievable scenes were being played out. No sooner had I changed a role of film than the camera's film counter zipped to the end.

Everyone in the University of Hawaii research team, people who have been investigating whales for years, looked incredulous and baldly surprised.

"Did you see that, Naka?"

"Of course. I got everything," I proudly answered, pointing at my film-exhausted camera.

The day's excitement went on until a thick New York steak that I consumed with some delicious California wine settled in my stomach, and I fell into a deep sleep in my bed late that night.

February 28

Gordon, the observer from the Olawalu field station, was out on the ocean for the first time this season. He had completely covered himself in clothing—long-sleeved shirt, long pants, and socks—because he planned to spend the entire day beneath the Pacific sun. He maneuvered the raft while rubbing sunscreen all over his face and hands, as we left the port of Lahaina.

During the morning we identified three pods and were quite content with the work we had done. As we headed toward the quiet off-shore waters to eat our lunch, we saw many whale-spouts reaching into the sky, against the background of the distant island. There was hardly a moment when we saw no sprays at all, for as one ceased another was just starting up.

"It's a giant pod," Gordon said quietly. We gave up any thought of lunch and set out at full throttle for the pod. The whales were spouting and submerging one after another. We could not even count their numbers. I guessed there were at least ten of them. The biggest pod I had seen before was composed of a female and its calf along with three escorts. Our raft gradually approached to within 300 meters of the pod. We discovered that another raft, also with a permit flag, was chasing after the pod to investigate. Unfortunately, we had to wait until they finished their work and left the pod.

Surrendering the raft to the ocean swells, we began our lunch of taro chips and apples. While eating, we continued to keep watch through our binoculars, wishing that the other raft would leave and the pod of whales would stay.

"Let's go for a swim," offered Gordon, and he jumped into the sea. Through the viewfinder of my camera, I noticed that the research craft had turned from the pod and was coming in our direction. Quickly, I yelled out, "The raft's quit the pod. Let's go!" Having cooled down his overheated body, Gordon hurried back to the raft. Still in his swimming trunks, he fired up the engine, and we sped full tilt toward the pod. We approached to within 100 meters and then 50 meters of the pod. After they finished catching their breaths, the whales submerged. The raft continued to close on the pod, and after seven minutes, one of the whales came up spouting just ten meters behind us.

Quickly, I turned around, readying my camera, when suddenly all around us were whales rising to the surface, spouting. We were completely surrounded by the pod; it was possible that a whale might accidentally come up right under us or strike us with its flukes. The whales were as much as 50 meters long, while our raft was only 3.5 meters long. These thoughts made my blood run cold, and Gordon seemed to share them. He changed the course of the raft so as to position us a little behind the pod.

When I looked down into the sea, there were giant black shapes moving along under the water. The pod was larger than just ten whales. Head slapping and fluke slapping, the pod swam in the direction of the island of Hawaii at about eight knots. It was quite an active group, but from the surface we could not make out just what the whales below us were up to.

After I had taken enough shots above the water, I became curious about what was going on under the surface, though in the face of the pod's speed and power I felt genuinely uncertain of my position. I asked Gordon if I might go into the water. He thought about it for a while and said, "Good luck." As I started to prepare myself for the dive, Gordon did likewise. He also showed Ronnie how to control the raft. Gordon told me that if anything happened to me while I was in the water, he would jump in to help. Feeling under terrific pressure, I straddled the side of the boat and got my breathing under control. Gordon, wearing fins and a face mask, maneuvered the raft toward the pod.

After about seven minutes of diving time, the first of the whales to surface appeared. At full speed, our raft moved in front of it. Just before the whale began to take its next breath, I dove into the water about fifteen meters ahead of it. As soon as I submerged, an enormous black shape passed on by. I chased after it at my greatest possible speed, but the whale, with tremendous power, rapidly sank away from me into the depths.

The next time I went down, I was seven or eight meters away from another whale. It had finished blowing and, bending its body like a jackknife, dove down with its back toward and slanting away from me. Off to the side, another whale chased after it. The water was transparent down to about twenty meters — not too good — so I could not see more than two whales at once. Whales suddenly

appeared before me and immediately disappeared into the dark beyond my vision. Within fifty meters all around me, there were over ten whales, but it was almost like an incredible fantasy. I struggled up to the raft and dove back again. I repeated this over and over, but it was impossible to take any photographs that could capture the entire pod underwater. I admitted defeat and returned my diving gear and underwater camera to the bottom of the raft.

Reflections on the Whale

"Gentle Giant." I like to use this phrase in referring to whales, not just because it sounds nice, but because of the impressions I have of them through my close association with some 150 humpbacks over the eight years since I became interested in whales.

From the whales' point of view, I have never been a friendly neighbor or close companion to them although we live on the same planet. To the whales, I suppose, I was an invader, coming unusually deep into their territory with the noises of motorboats or small aircraft. I was a strange and unidentifiable creature, who did not swim very well, but eagerly drew close to them, with legs flapping and a weird object of some kind attached to my front.

Indeed, there were only three whales that came close to the rafts I have been aboard. Most of them hated the approaching boat, changing again and again the direction of their swimming or remaining underwater longer in order to avoid it.

When I dove into the water from the raft to photograph them underwater, many whales went deeper into the sea or veered away at the sound of my dive. After I discovered that the whales were trying to avoid me, I waited for them to draw closer to the raft with the engine shut off. I was also careful to slip noiselessly into the water whenever I dove. I did not swim and chase after them, but waited for them to come close to me as I floated like a log.

On one occasion a calf became interested in a piece of driftwood and came to within two meters of it. When I began to photograph the scene, the mother whale hurried up to the calf as though she were scolding a child. She swam between me and her calf, and I quickly moved back to avert the near miss. The mother whale and her calf then swam out of my field of view as though nothing had happened. This was the only instance in which I had to get out of the way of an approaching whale.

There was another time when we found our entire raft was on a whale's back, riding high in the air. I still do not know how it happened—whether our raft went over the whale's back or whether the whale accidentally rose up under the raft. Again, the surprised parties were the human beings, while the indifferent whale nonchalantly swam away.

Although the whales, with the tremendous power hidden in their huge bodies, were quite capable of easily knocking away the raft or me with their flukes, I never felt in such danger. Once after I had dived into the water and ended up, quite by chance, directly in front of a group of whales, they avoided a collision by moving away.

In fact, I felt most insecure and hesitant while still in the raft, before diving in. But once in the ocean, with the whales in plain sight, my insecurity evaporated. All I saw were these huge, tranquil, and sympathetic creatures, who are most accurately described as "Gentle Giants."

"Let's show these whales to our children and grandchildren." Five years ago I read this statement in Hawaii. I still recall that when I read it, the blood drained from my body. Years from now, I thought, when I have grandchildren who are grown, will whales still be swimming through this ocean where once I rafted around, in such excitement, searching for them?

There are species that my grandparents could have come upon easily that are now on the verge of extinction. Only in very secluded ocean redoubts can they be found. This knowledge fills me with apprehension for the future of these gentle giants.

Right: Some whales act independently and live alone. In most cases they are young males and evince a strong sense of curiosity. ►

SWIMMING IN THE OCEAN

Above: Pilot fish accompany a diving whale.

Right: After this whale passed by our raft, I dove into the water right after it. ▶

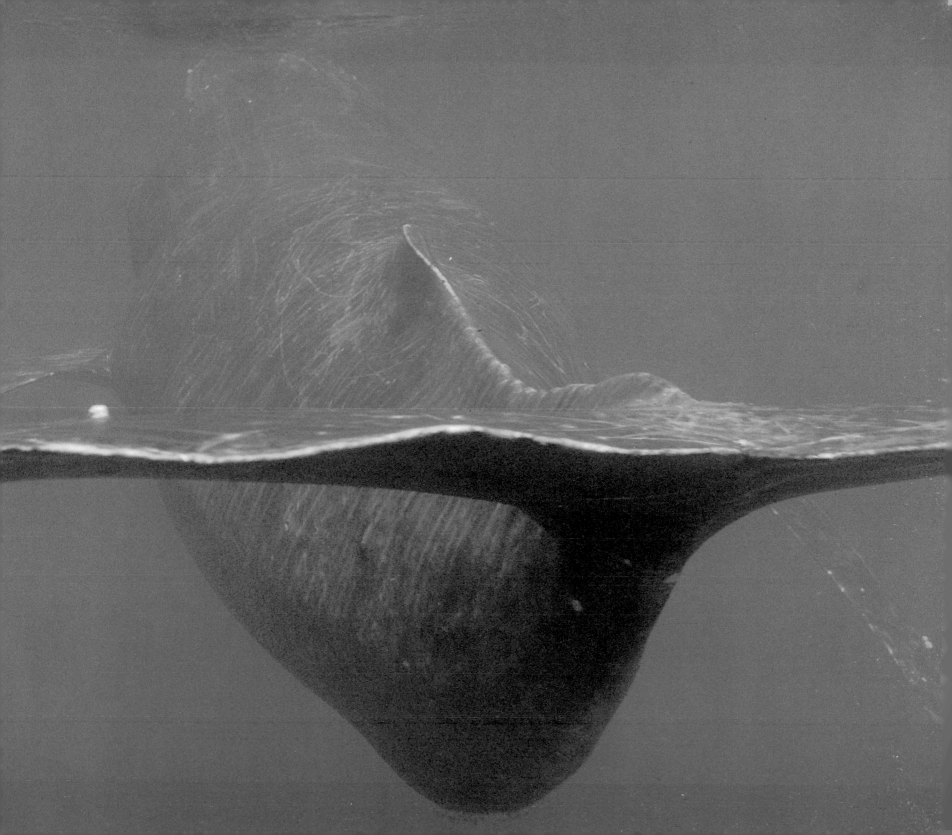

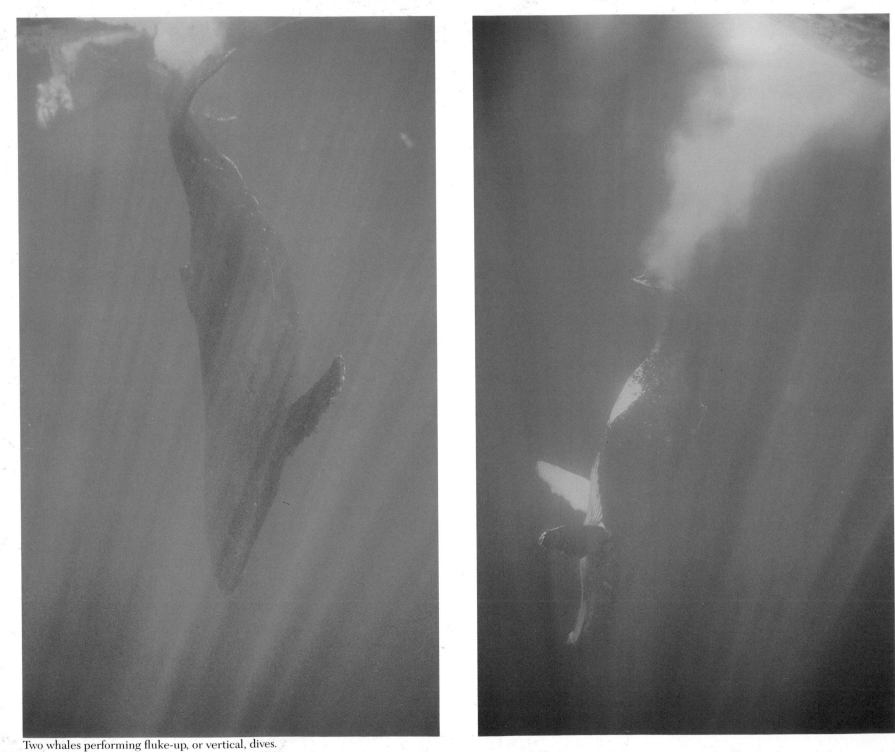

Two whales performing fluke-up, or vertical, dives.

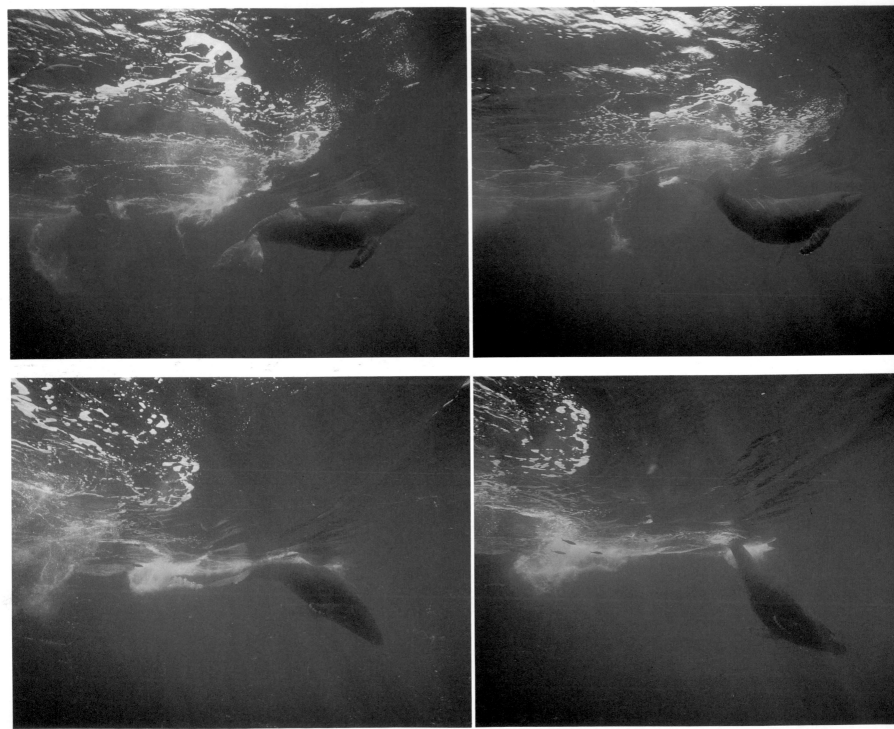

Preceding page and six photos above: While swimming just under the surface of the water, the whale spouts several times, gains control of its breathing, and prepares itself for a long submersion.

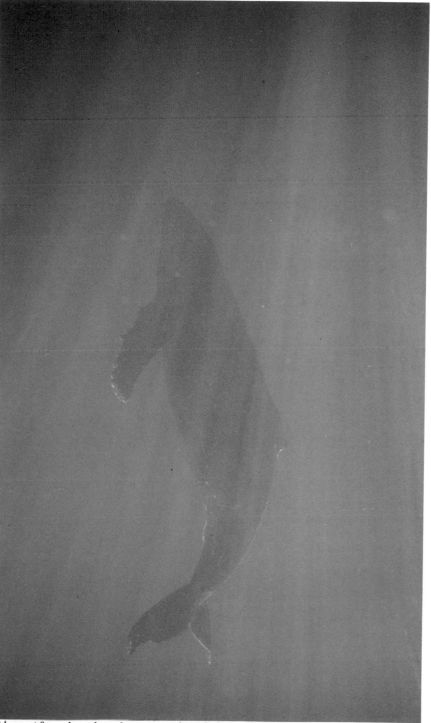

Above: After a lengthy submersion, this whale heads for the surface. *Following page:* A "giant pod," or group.

Opposite and above: In this "giant pod" the whales are threatening one another by taking short submersions, surfacing, and spouting one after another.

A HUGE BODY VIBRANT WITH LIFE

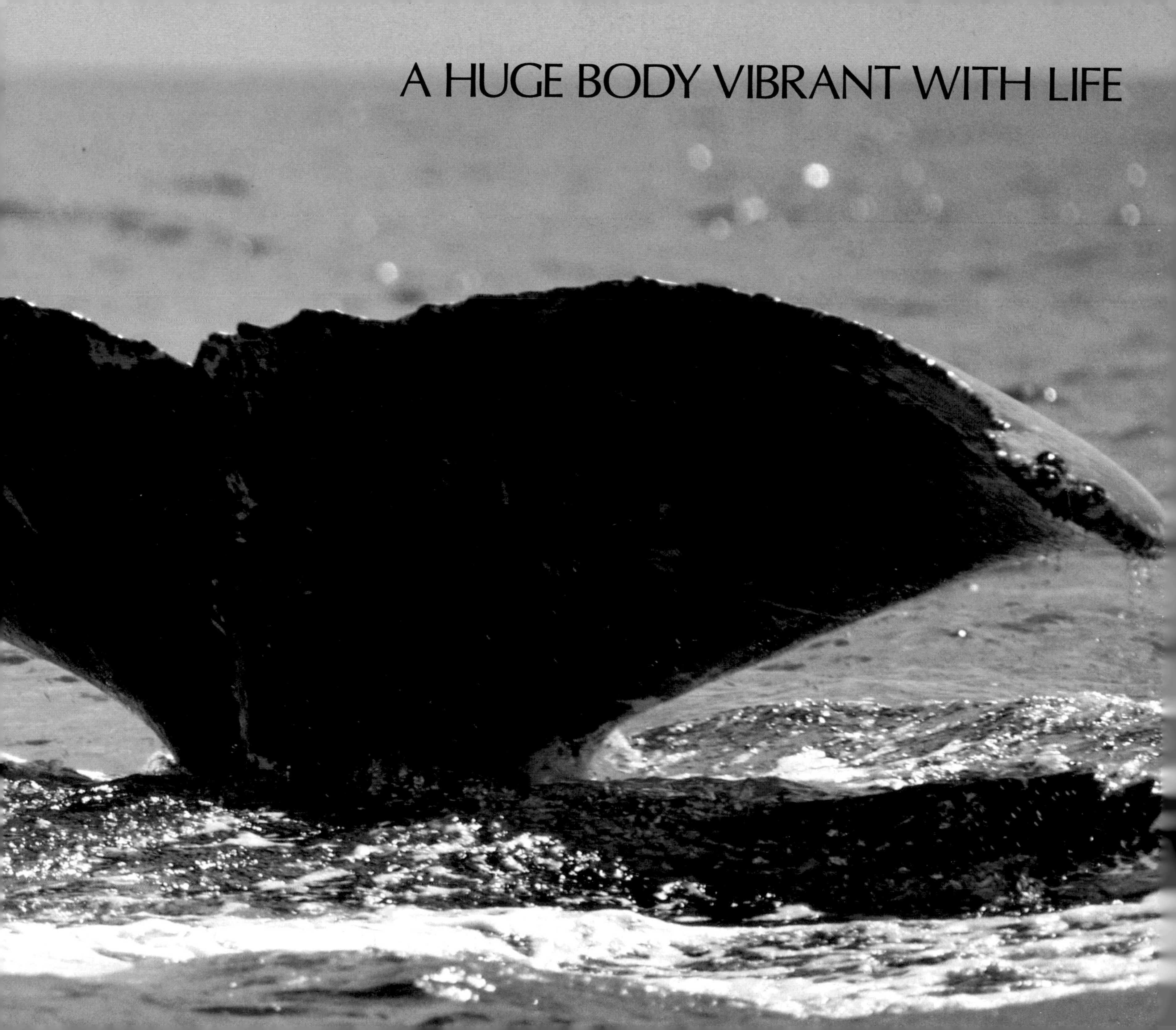

Preceding page: The flukes of two whales break the water simultaneously.

Above and opposite: Two whales engage in a magnificent duel.

Above and opposite: Two whales threaten one another: one breaches while the other lunges with a mouthful of seawater, trying to make itself look bigger.

Fluke-swish, waving flukes in the air.

Slapping the water with the back of the fluke.

Slapping the water with the top of the fluke.

Fluke-slap.

Above and right: When a whale breaches, it first breaks through the surface of the water, raising its head and spouting. Then, when half of the body is out of the water, the whale raises its flippers and swings them behind its back, as though doing a backstroke.

Above and opposite: Breaching.

Opposite: One whale climbs over another, which is lying belly-up. ►

This whale is "spying," keeping watch around itself with its head above water.

Two whales lying on their sides threaten one another.

28

◄ *Opposite:* This whale stretches the wrinkle under its chin to fill its mouth with seawater in order to appear as big and threatening as possible.

Above: A whale leans its head over another whale's flukes.

Above and opposite: With its body, a whale pushes up the lower half of another whale which is on the surface above it.

◄ *Opposite:* An underwater fight. Both whales have scratched each other's bodies with their barnacles.

Above: Three whales swim into my view at once.

Above and right: A calf swimming close to its mother.

◄ *Opposite:* Calf and mother.

Above: A calf engaging in "spying" behavior.

A calf breaches again and again as if playing.

Following page: A calf and mother. The calf's white flippers and white patches behind its eyes are features used in identification.

The round surface pattern that forms after a fluke-up dive is called the whale's "footprint."

PARENTS AND OFFSPRING

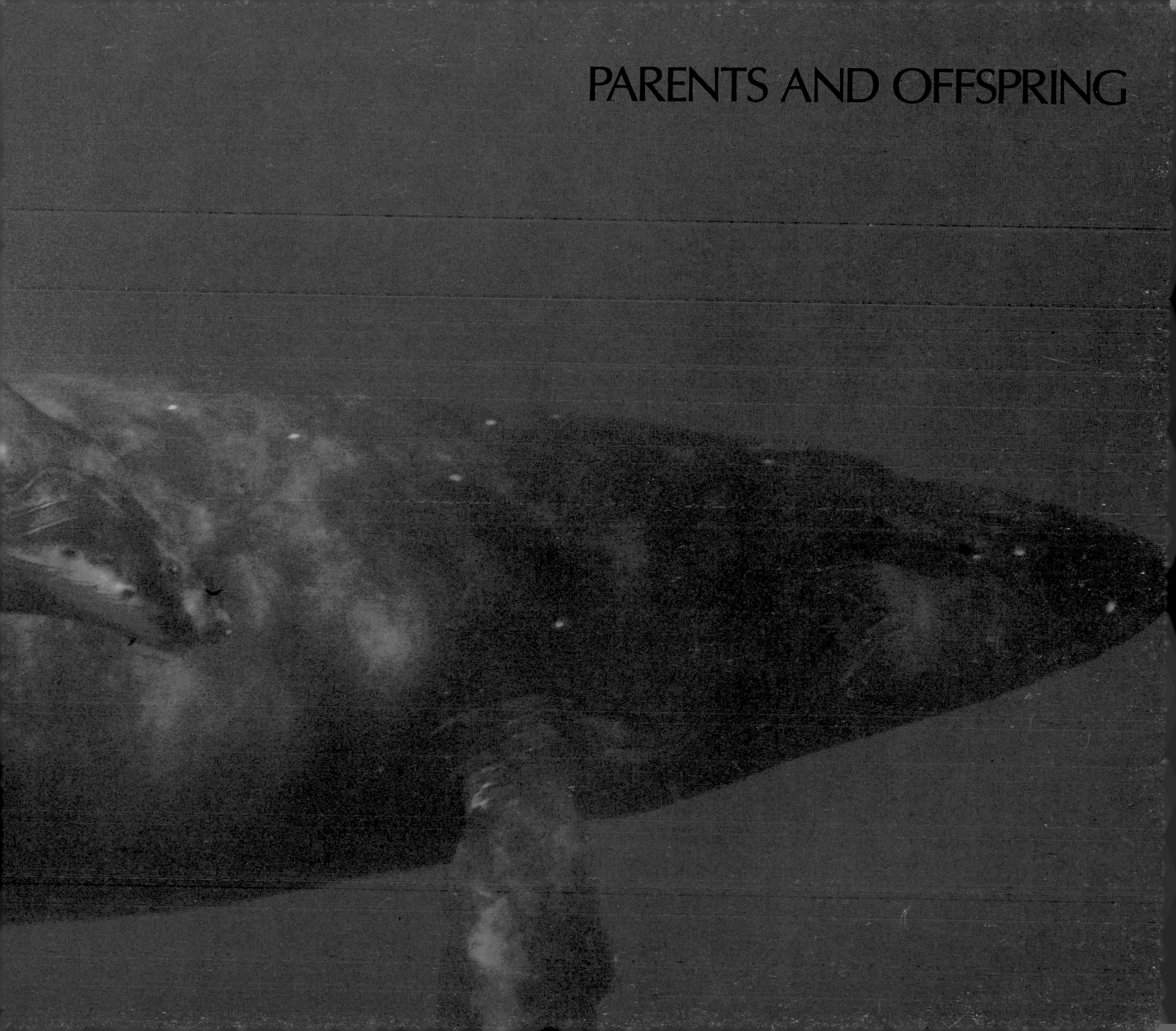

Page 44: A mother whale protects her newborn calf by keeping it over her head.

Page 45: A calf swimming close to and over its parents.

Page 46: A curious calf swims close to me, leaving its parent, who quickly interposes itself between us.

Page 47: A slightly bigger calf, about a year old, and its mother.

Right: A male escort swims under a mother and her calf, as if to protect them. ▶

◄ *Opposite:* Mother, calf, and escort.

Flippers extending out of the water.

Above: This whale holds its flipper above the water while making a turn.
Right: I took this photo of the whale's blowhole when it picked the raft up out of the water on its back.

◄ *Opposite and above:* Part of a whale's head. The knobs on its head are peculiar to humpbacks.

The shape of the whales' flukes and their patterns are used for identification.
Sometimes the flukes have been bitten by sharks or orcas, or injured in fights.

◄ *Left:* A whale swimming in the dawn ocean.

Above: This whale's spouting shows up clearly against the island.

A series of fluke-up dives.

Above: In order to get this photo, I chased the whale until sunset. *Following page:*
A silhouette in the intense afternoon sunshine.